CONTENTS

INTRODUCTION

A mass of floating butter muslin contrasts with the crisp white cotton bedcovers and softens the austere lines of the black metal bed frame, whilst the luxuriant bunches of silk roses add a touch of sophistication.

The master bedroom is probably – in living terms – the most important room in the house after the kitchen and the family room. Historically, the main bedroom was always granted great status – as can be seen in the many châteaux and country houses which open their rooms to the public. Huge expense would be lavished on the bed chamber, with ornate curtaining, a large fireplace, and with the bed taking pride of place. We find ornate and elaborate bed 'dressings', such as the 'corona' or 'tester', with their intricate designs and lavish use of gilt. Bed upholstery used only the best fabrics and passementerie, and this seemed to be as much a symbol of importance and wealth as the house and grounds.

The bedroom is the most personal room in the house and to a large extent the most important room in our lives. It is in the bedroom that some of the major events in our lives take place - most of us were conceived in the bedroom, many were born in them and we like to think that we will end our days in our own bed.

When we are tired and weary we seek the solace of the bedroom, and so the decoration should be more restful than stimulating. We are likely to spend longer periods of time in bed if we are unwell and then a peaceful environment is essential.

marvellous for guest rooms.

Measure a four-poster carefully to make sure that it does not look completely out of proportion in the room. A high brass or wooden bed in a small room might look fine with little other decoration, but it will be difficult to find an easy chair or a dressing table which balance and do not appear to be dwarfed by the bed.

Children grow up very quickly and consequently their bedrooms need to be thought through carefully. Fashionable cartoons or television series today will be outdated within a very short period of time. Children's bedrooms will first be playrooms and then studies as the teenage years and exams loom. Simple furniture which can be adapted as needs change should be researched. Strong primary colours may be good for play and work, but might be too stimulating for sleep.

I have tried to cover a cross section of different styles and designs within this book to suit as many situations, budgets and tastes as possible. Do not be daunted if you feel that your rooms are too small or too ordinary: a well-dressed bed is as important in a small apartment as in a grand house, and the general approach to design much the same.

As always, the essence of good design is not how much you can spend on a room but what you have done with the materials available. Above all, start your project with enthusiasm, take time and great care over the making up, and design your own individual details for that extra special finishing touch.

The colours you select for the bedroom should always be chosen instinctively as those you would be happy to live with for hours on end, day and night if need be. The colours generally preferred will be soft, often creams and/or whites with pinks, pale apricots or light blues. If deeper colours are chosen they will almost always be earthy tones – soft terracotta, olive greens, pinky earth reds.

The bed itself will always be the main piece of furniture in the bedroom, principally because of its size in relation to the room. If you are able to choose a new bed, choose carefully. A small double will be fine for the first few years but are not so much fun with a child lying crossways between you! Twin beds zip-linked will provide the solution for many couples. These are also

BASIC TECHNIQUES

STITCHES

Start and finish all stitching with a double stitch, never use a knot.

Hemming stitch

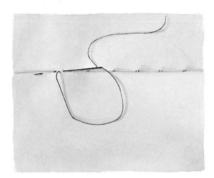

This stitch is used along hems. Each stitch should be approximately 1.5 cm (⅝ in) in length. Slide the needle through the folded hem, pick up two threads of the main fabric, and push the needle directly back into the fold.

Herringbone stitch

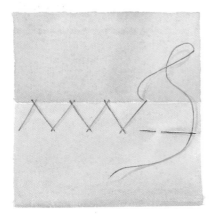

Herringbone stitch is used over any raw edge which is then covered by another fabric. It is worked in the opposite direction to all other stitches. Each stitch should be about 3 cm (1¼ in) for hems and 8 cm (3¼ in) for side turnings. Stitch into the hem, from right to left, approximately 1.5 cm (⅝ in) to the right make a stitch into the fabric picking up two threads. Pull through and stitch 1.5 cm (⅝ in) to the right making a stitch into the hem.

Ladder stitch

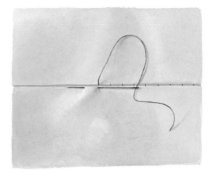

Ladder stitch is used to join two folded edges invisibly together. Slide the needle along the fold 5 mm (¼ in) and straight into the fold opposite. Slide along for 5 mm (¼ in) and back into the first fold, again directly opposite.

Long stitch

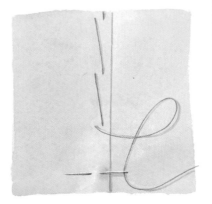

Long stitch is the most effective stitch for interlined curtains as it holds the interlining tight to the main fabric on the side turnings.

Make a horizontal stitch approximately 1 cm (⅜ in) across. Bring the thread down diagonally by about 4 cm (1½ in) and repeat.

Slip stitch

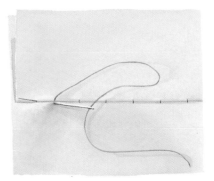

This stitch is used to sew on linings. Always use a colour thread which matches the main fabric. Make each stitch 1.5 cm (⅝ in). Slide the needle through the main fabric and pick up two threads of the lining. Push the needle back into the main fabric exactly opposite and slide through a further 1.5 cm (⅝ in).

Lock stitch

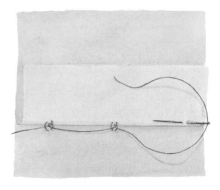

This stitch holds linings, interlinings and fabrics together, preventing them from separating, but still allowing some degree of movement. Always use thread that blends with the main fabric and the lining when stitching lining to interlining. Fold back the lining, secure the thread to the lining and make a small stitch in the main fabric just below. Make a large loop approximately 10 cm (4 in) long (slightly shorter for smaller items) and make a small stitch in the lining inside this loop. Stitch into the main fabric. Allow the stitch to remain slightly loose.

Buttonhole stitch

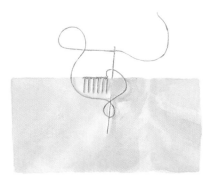

Work from left to right with the raw edge uppermost. Push the needle from the back to the front, 3 mm (⅛ in) below the edge. Twist the thread around the needle and pull the needle through, carefully tightening the thread so that it knots on the edge.

Blanket stitch

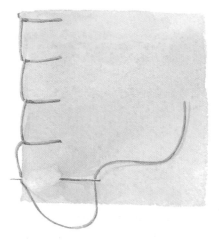

Originally used to neaten the raw edges of woollen blankets, it is now mainly decorative. It is most comfortable worked from the side with the edge towards you. Push the needle from the front to the back, about 6 mm (¼ in) from the edge (also this measurement will vary with large or small items). Hold the thread from the last stitch under the needle and pull up to make a loop on the edge.

PINNING

When pinning two layers of fabric together or piping on to fabric, always use horizontal and vertical pins to keep the fabric in place from both directions. The horizontal pins need to be removed just before the machine foot reaches them and the vertical ones – or cross pins – can remain in place, so the fabrics are held together the whole time.

SEAMS

Flat seam

The most common and straightforward seam for normal use. With right sides together, pin 1.5–2 cm (⅝–¾ in) in from the edge at 10 cm (4 in) intervals. Pin cross pins halfway between each seam pin. These cross pins will remain in place while you are stitching to prevent the fabrics from slipping.

Once machine-stitched, open

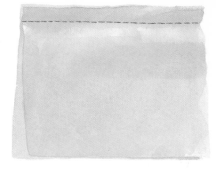

the seam flat and press it from the back. Turn it over and press from the front. Turn it back over once again and press from the back, under each flap, to remove the pressed ridge line.

French seam

This type of seam is very neat and leaves no raw edges. Use for sheer fabrics or any occasion when the seam might be visible.

Pin the fabrics together with the wrong sides facing. Stitch 5 mm (¼ in) from the raw edges. Trim and flip the fabric over, bringing the right sides together. Pin again, 1 cm (⅜ in) from the stitched edge and stitch along this line to enclose the raw edges. Press from the right side, always pressing the seam in one direction only.

Flat fell seam

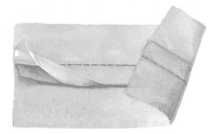

Use for neatening seams of heavier weight fabrics. Pin the fabrics together with the right sides facing and stitch 1.5–3 cm (⅝–1¼ in) from the raw edges. Trim one seam to just under half. Fold the other over to enclose the raw edge. Press down. Stitch close to the fold line.

MITRED CORNERS

This technique creates a flat and neat finish to corners.

When sides and hems are equal

1. Press the side seam over and the hem up, to the measurements given. Position a temporary pin exactly through the point of the corner.

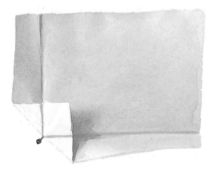

2. Open out the folds and turn in the corner at a 45° angle, with the pin at the centre of the foldline.

3. Fold the hem up and the sides in again along the original fold lines. Keep the pin on the point and make sure the fabric is firmly tucked into the folded lines.

When sides and hems are unequal

Even when this is the case, you can still achieve a neat corner. Follow step 1 as above, but when you reach step 2, the corner will not be folded to a 45° angle.

Instead, the corner will need to be angled away, towards the hem, leaving a longer fold on the side turnings so that the raw edges meet when the mitre is finished.

MAKING TIES

Ties are used throughout soft furnishings. They can be used to close duvets, tie bed cushions, or to secure a headboard cover. For curtains, they can tie a heading to a pole.

Folded ties

Cut a strip of fabric four times the width of your finished tie and 3 cm (1¼ in) longer. Press one short end under by 1 cm (⅜ in) and both sides to the middle. Press in half, and stitch close to the fold line.

Rouleau ties

Cut a strip of fabric four times the width of your finished tie and 3 cm (1¼ in) longer. Fold in half lengthwise, right sides together, enclosing a piece of cord which is longer than the strip of fabric. Stitch along the short side to secure the cord firmly. Stitch along the length, 2 mm (⅛ in) towards the raw edge from the centre.

Trim the fabric across the corner, pull the cord through, at the same time turning the fabric right side out. Cut off the cord. Press the raw edge under and slipstitch with small stitches.

PIPING

If piping is to be used in straight lines then it will be easier to handle straight. If it is to be bent around corners, then it should be cut on the cross. For 4 mm (⅛ in) piping cord cut 4 cm (1½ in) wide strips. All joins should be made on the cross to minimise bulk.

To cut on the straight
Cut lengths as long as possible. Hold two strips, butt the ends together and trim away both corners at 45°. Hold together and flip the top one over. Stitch together where the pieces cross.

To cut on the cross

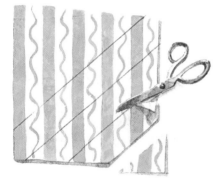

With the fabric flat on the table fold one bottom corner as if making a 30 cm (12 in) square. Cut along the fold line. Mark pencil lines from this cut edge at 4 cm (1½ in) intervals, and cut along these lines. Hold two pieces, butting the ends together as if making a continuous strip. Flip the top one over and hold. Machine stitch together where the two fabrics cross.

Making up and pinning on
Press seams flat and cut away excess corners. Fold in half along the length and insert the piping cord. Machine stitch to encase, approximately 2 mm (⅛ in) from the cord. Keep the fabric folded exactly in half.

Always pin piping so that the raw edges line up exactly with the raw edges of the main fabric.

To bend piping around curves, snip into the stitching line. To pipe around a right angle, stop pinning 1.5 cm (⅝ in) from the corner, snip the piping right to the stitching line, fold the piping to 90° and start pinning 1.5 cm (⅝ in) on the adjacent side.

Joining
To join piping, overlap by approximately 6 cm (2¼ in) and cut away excess. Unpick the casing on one side and cut away the cord so that the two ends butt up. Fold the piping fabric across at a 45° angle and cut along this fold. Fold under 1 cm (⅝ in) and pin securely before stitching.

BINDING

Binding one edge
1. Cut the binding strips to the width required. Join the strips on the cross for the required length.

2. Pin the binding to the fabric, right sides together and stitch slightly less than 1.5 cm (⅝ in) from the raw edges.

3. Neaten the raw edges to slightly less than 1.5 cm (⅝ in). Press from the front, pressing the binding away from the main fabric. Fold the binding to the back, measuring the edge to 1.5 cm (⅝ in), keeping the fabric tucked firmly into the fold and pin at approximately 8 cm (3¼ in) intervals. Turn over to the back and herringbone stitch the edge of the binding to the main fabric, or fold under again.

Binding a corner
If you need to bind a corner, mitre the binding. Stop pinning just short of the corner by the width of the finished binding. Fold the binding back on itself to make a sharp 45° angle and pin across this fold line.

Continue to pin on the adjacent side, the same distance from the edge. Stitch the binding on, stopping right on the pin and secure stitching. Begin stitching again at the same point, on the adjacent side. Press to mitre, and fold the fabric to the back, mitring the corner in the opposite direction to relieve the bulk.

MEASURING AND ESTIMATING

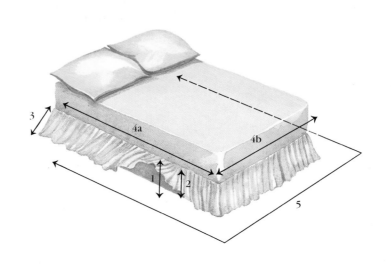

Although there are 'standard' bed sizes these do vary slightly from manufacturer to manufacturer and often greatly from country to country. When buying fabric or bedding always take your own measurements to compare rather than relying absolutely on the usual single, double, queen and king descriptions. If you need to purchase a new bed, or have ordered one, use the manufacturer's measurement for estimating purposes but wait until you have the bed to measure exactly – even one centimetre or half an inch can make a lot of difference to the drape of a bed valance. Mattress depths too can vary by as much as 15 cm (6 in).

Always measure the bed without bedding and, where necessary, with summer and winter weight bedding to show you the allowances needed for the finished articles.

Bed sizes

	width	length
single	100 cm	190 cm
	(3 ft 3 in)	(6 ft 3 in)
double	135 cm	190 cm
	(4 ft 6 in)	(6 ft 3 in)
queen	150 cm	200 cm
	(5 ft)	(6 ft 6 in)
king	180 cm	200 cm
	(6 ft)	(6 ft 6 in)
twin,	200 cm	200 cm
zipped	(6 ft 6 in)	(6 ft 6 in)

BED VALANCES

The primary function of a bed valance is to cover the part of the bed underneath the mattress. Some bed frames are works of art in their own right and need not be covered, but often unattractive material covering the divan base and any ugly metal or wooden bed frames can be covered with a skirt.

First, a 'platform' of lining, calico or other inexpensive but sturdy fabric is made to fit exactly over the bed base, under the mattress and then the 'skirt' which may be straight, pleated or gathered is stitched to the platform.

The length of the skirt will be determined primarily by the height of the bed base, but can be made overlong to drape on to the floor. If you are using the space under the bed for storage, either open or with divan drawers, you will need to be able to lift the valance for easy access. In this case, a gathered skirt will be practical but if you prefer a tailored style, then make false pleats with flaps of fabric which can be lifted easily.

To fit a valance to a bed with posts or footboards you will need to make three separate skirts, one for each side and one for the end, leaving space at the corner for the platform to fit around the leg.

Measure (see above)
1. Top of bed base to the floor.
2. Top of bed base to the bottom of the bed base.
3. Valance skirt drape from top of bed base to the floor.
4. Valance platform length (4a) and width (4b).
5. Measure around the end of the bed and the two sides.

Estimate
Platform: Allow to join your fabric widths. Seam as necessary to keep a centre width of fabric with joins at either side.
Border: Allow three cuts of the main fabric 15 cm (6 in) plus 2 cm (⅝ in) seam allowances for two lengths and one width.
Skirt: Allow fullness for pleating the whole skirt or corners only, or for gathering. Divide the total by the width of your fabric to find the number of cuts needed. Add 6 cm (2¼ in) to the skirt length for seam allowances.

BEDCOVERS

Bedcovers fall into two general categories – fitted and throwover, both of which may be made to fall to the floor or to stop short to show the bed legs.

All bedcovers need to be measured over your normal bedlinen, which will alter depending upon the time of year. Throwover covers may be plainly finished with a straight binding or border, or with more detail such as fringes which need to be considered when measurements are taken. All four corners may be square or the ends can be rounded. Fitted covers are made in two pieces, a top to fit the top of the bed and a skirt stitched around the three free sides.

Pillow allowances

Pillows need to be either tucked in tidily or covered with decorative covers and displayed on top of the bedcover.

There are three ways to make allowances for pillows which lay under the cover.

● Make a separate flap of fabric stitched to the top of the bedcover, long enough to fold up, over the pillows and then to tuck underneath.

● Extend the width and length to allow the bedcover to be tucked in under the pillows and to drop down over the sides (Fig i).

● To include a gusset, measure the height and length of your pillows and cut a template to fit. Add seam allowances and stitch to the bedcover top as shown (Fig ii).

Measure

For throwover:

1. Bedcover length (short to cover the top of the valance or bed frame, or long to reach to the floor).

2. Bedcover width (short or long).

For fitted:

3. The top of the bed, both length and width.

4. Around the sides and end of the bed for the skirt total.

Estimate

If a throwover, measure the width and length as described above. If fitted, measure the top only. Divide the total width by the width of your fabric to find the number of cuts needed. Always allow the centre panel to be a full width of fabric with seams to either side.

Make allowance for pillow flaps or tuck-ins as required (see pillow allowances, above). For a fitted cover, allow fullness for gathers or pleats and divide by the fabric width to find the number of cuts needed. Seam allowances of 2 cm (¾ in) for the top and 4 cm (1½ in) for the hem should be added.

Standard duvet sizes

	width	length
single	140 cm (56 in)	200 cm (78 in)
double	200 cm (78 in)	200 cm (78 in)
queen	210 cm (86 in)	220 cm (90 in)
king	240 cm (96 in)	220 cm (90 in)
superking	260 cm (104 in)	220 cm (90 in)

Fig i

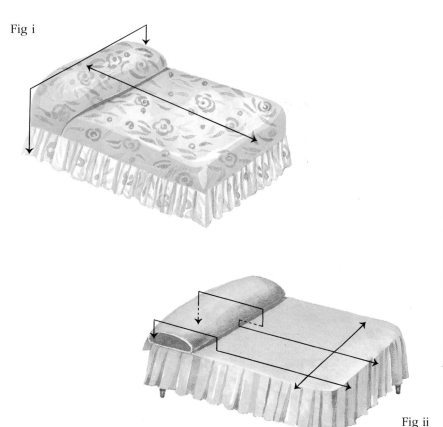

Fig ii

VALANCES

A new look for the most traditional
fabrics – denim, gingham, tartan,
Normandy stripes and Madras checks:
ostensibly for a teenage bedroom, but
who would not be comfortable
sleeping here?

Bed valances are essential bedroom soft furnishings which hide the base of modern divans and the metal bars and springs of antique metal, wooden or brass-framed beds. Even if you have a full length throwover bedcover, it is unlikely that the divan or bed base will be attractive enough to leave uncovered when the bedcover is pulled back, or not in use. Antique beds, usually high off the floor, provide valuable storage space for spare linen; if you are fortunate enough to have antique trunks you can make a feature of this space, but a fabric valance may provide welcome cover for less attractive items.

Bed valances do take time to make and involve a considerable amount of fabric, so it is well worth choosing a good fabric which will last the lifetime of the bed, finishing the valance well and adding interesting details.

Choose valance fabrics to work with your overall room scheme but especially with your headboard and bedcover. Imagine you choose a stripe for the valance and headboard, you could then select duvet covers or bedcovers from many options. Experiment by using plain colours which pick up the tones of the stripes: for the summer, plain white cotton, a floral print in similar tones or a patchwork of florals, stripes and plains. Or use strong colour and textural contrasts: perhaps Mediterranean blues with strong yellows, adding lilac and aquamarine details; Madras checked cottons with denim and crisp white linen; or black and white ticking with red/blue and green tartan blankets.

Bed valances are generally pleated, gathered or straight, with any number of variations added. Valances may need to be split at the corners to accommodate the ends of bed legs, or they may need false pleats which form flaps for easy access to divan drawers. However valances are designed, they should be lined and made full enough to give body.

MAKING UP

Measure the bed base from the top to the floor. Note any unusual projections, bedposts etc, which might prevent the valance fitting easily, especially on old beds and four posters. Measure the length and width of the bed base (the platform), then the position of any bedhead fixings. Make a template of the corners at both the top and bottom ends of the bed base. Decide how long you want the valance to be and how full. I always allow three times fullness depending on the weight of the fabric. Allow at least 1 cm (³/₈ in) for a frilled skirt to drape to the floor. Plan the widths of fabric needed. Allow seam allowances – 2 cm (³/₄ in) all around the platform and 6 cm (2¼ in) for the skirt.

1. Cut the skirt widths of the main fabric and lining; join. Press the seams flat. Make three strips of fabric 15 cm (6 in) wide, two the length of the bed and one the width. Cut and join lining to make the platform, the width and length of the bed plus 2 cm (³/₄ in) seam allowance all around.

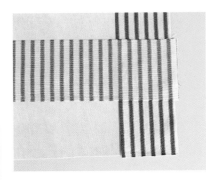

2. Press under 1.5 cm (⁵/₈ in) all along one side of each of the strips for the platform border. Pin all three pieces on to the platform. Fold the side pieces back at the corners to mitre the joins. Stitch all around the inside of these strips.

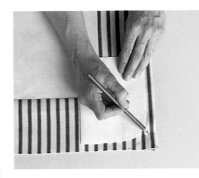

3. Place the corner template on to the platform, add the seam allowance and cut round.

4. Pin piping all around the three sides and 15 cm (6 in) around the top corners along the bedhead.

5. Stitch the skirt lining to the main fabric, right sides together, with a 1.5 cm (⁵/₈ in) seam allowance. Press from the front, pressing the fabric towards the lining. Turn over and press from the back, folding along the fabric to show 2–2.5 cm (³/₄–1 in).

6. Pin all along the top edge and trim the lining to match the main fabric exactly. Press the fabric and lining ends in and slipstitch together. Stitch a double gathering thread all around 1.5 cm (⁵/₈ in) and 2 cm (³/₄ in) from the top.

7. Divide the valance into 10 equal sections and mark each with coloured tacks. Mark the three sides of the platform into 10 equal sections. Pin the skirt to the platform, matching these points. Pull the threads to gather each section and pin the gathering line to the piping line.

8. Stitch all around. Neaten the seam and press. Stitch tape into each corner so that you can secure the valance to each bed leg. Lift the mattress from the bed. Place the valance on top of the bed base and tie the tapes around the legs.

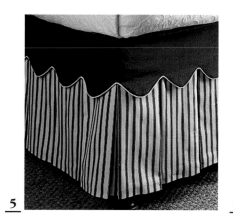

EDGINGS AND FINISHES

1. For a pretty country finish, cut the valance a little shorter than floor length to allow a picot lace or broderie anglais trim. The edge was first piped with 20 mm (¾ in) ribbon in the deeper blue, and the lining slip stitched over to cover the raw edges. This style of valance looks good cut 10–15 cm (4–6 in) short for antique brass or iron frame beds.

2. Binding the hem adds an attractive detail but also weights the skirt, allowing it to fall well whether it drapes on to the floor or hangs short. Cut 6 cm (2¼ in) strips on the cross for checks or stripes, but on the straight for plain fabrics. Stitch right sides together along the hemline, 1.4 cm (just under ⅝ in) from the raw edges. Press binding to the back leaving a neat 1.5 cm (⅝ in) edge. Fold the raw edge under and slipstitch to the stitching line. If the valance is lined, tack stitch the lining and main fabric together before adding the binding.

3. Double valances are always interesting – use stripes or checks cut on the cross, two patterned fabrics with similar colour tones or two contrasting plain fabrics. Two separate valances are made up and joined together with the gathering thread. To reduce bulk, the under-valance is made from a single layer, cut to floor length, with just a border of main fabric added to the front. Cut the border to the chosen depth, adding 10 cm (4 in) for turnings. Stitch the right side of the border to the wrong side of the lining hem, press to the front, press the raw edge under 1 cm (⅜ in) and stitch to the under-valance, close to the fold line.

4. Pipe or bind one or both of the valances with contrasting fabric.

5. Allow three times fullness for box-pleated valances and pleat up so that they open at each corner. The flat scalloped top was made up, piped, lined and stitched to the pleated valance along the top before joining to the piped edge of the valance platform.

6. Stitch any closely woven, preshrunk ribbon or braid to the main fabric before making up. Place the ribbon carefully, considering the depth of valance, the depth of the ribbon and the bedcovers which will be used.

BEDCOVERS

Green and white roses are restful and sophisticated. Natural linen with a rich green stripe and deep green glazed linen complete the fabric selection.

Traditionally, most bedding consisted of sheets and blankets topped with a down cover and counterpane. Although fine linen sheets with the very best cotton or wool blankets still provide perhaps the most luxurious sleep, the majority of today's beds need to be easy to make and care for, combining a mixture of sheets, duvets, comforters and bedcovers.

As the bedcover is almost always the most dominant soft furnishing in the bedroom, it is well worth careful consideration. For this reason, it is fun to use several bedcovers together. Perhaps a plain cover with two plaid throws folded over; a plain comforter with a patterned bedcover folded back; checks, plain and florals mixed in harmony; or tweeds and printed paisley with velvet. Or make a bedcover with more than one fabric – experiment with patchworked pieces in a traditional design or sew together squares of complementary fabrics and border with braids. Quilting a bedcover adds variety; while adding a separate skirt offers the chance to use contrast edges and piping or a contrasting frill.

As we tend to move house more often, a full-sized bedcover is probably still important as a cover-all allowing non-matching bedlinen chosen for different reasons to be used underneath. If your budget allows, choose a fresh, light-weight cover for the summer and a heavier, winter bedcover which may or may not be used to sleep under but which becomes an attractive feature for whatever mix of bedding is underneath.

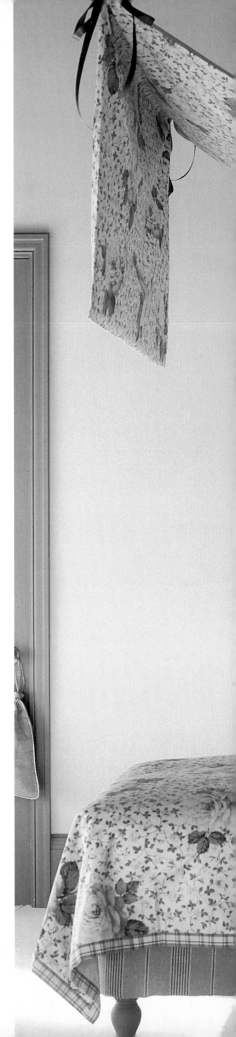

Always try to use a large flat area to make bedcovers – it is important that the layers do not move against each other during the making process.

MAKING UP

1. Join the cut lengths of fabric together, always keeping a full width in the centre. Press the seams flat.

2. If you have chosen to shape the bottom corners, mark out the bed size on to the fabric, allowing 5 cm (2 in) each way for bedding underneath. Using a long ruler, measure from the bottom bed corners to the length decided, adding 3 cm (1¼ in) for the turnings. With the end of the ruler still on the bed corner, continue to measure at 3-4 cm (1¼-1½ in) intervals and mark with pins.

Join the pins up with a light pencil line and carefully cut around this curve.

3. If you are using interlining, cut the corners to match, place on to the wrong side of the fabric and lock stitch the seams together.

4. Fold the fabric over 3 cm (1¼ in) all around and herringbone stitch using stitches about 32 cm (12 in) in length. Place the lining over and lock stitch.

5. Score the lining along the edge of the bedcover and trim 1 cm (⅜ in) inside this line. Fold the lining under and slipstitch.

FOUR POSTERS AND FOOTBOARDS

The bedcovers for any bed which has legs or a footboard at the end will need to be cut or shaped to accommodate the obstruction. If at all possible, shape or cut below the mattress so that the cover will push down over the corner and hold the linen underneath in place. You will need to measure carefully and mark accurately on the bedcover the point at which any split will start and finish. It is sometimes easier to fit the made-up bedcover on to the bed with all bedding in place before taking the scissors to it.

Remember to add 2 cm (¾ in) for your seam allowance when cutting. Finish the cut out corner in the same manner as the bedcover sides and hem - shown here with a contrast bound edge. Or if the bedcover has a more decorative edging such as frills, scalloped shaping or a passementerie trim, simply self pipe around the two sides of the square. Slipstitch the lining in place with very small stitches as this corner will receive more pushing and pulling than the others.

PATCHWORK BEDCOVER

A patchworked bedcover must be the ideal way to use up all of those soft furnishings off-cuts which are too large to throw away but too small to be really useful. With this type of patchwork there needs to be some colour co-ordination and a common colour running throughout, with a good variety of ancillary colours.

Predominantly yellow, this bedcover has many tones of greens with blues, lilacs and corals to supplement, and a good mix of prints and patterns. Log cabin patchwork is one of the simplest to follow and has the advantage that a very passable machined version can be made as long as you are careful to take consistent seam allowances. The bound edge gives a crisp finish; lining with a small geometric or stripe is more interesting than plain off-white.

QUILTING

Elaborate quilting should be sent to a specialist quilting company, but straightforward machined squares can be quilted with the aid of a domestic machine or a simple pattern might even be hand stitched.

The fabric should be quilted after it has been joined, but before any further making up. Polyester wadding is easily available in varied weights – a 100 g (4 oz) weight is suitable for average use, but 150 g (6 oz) gives a plumper look and shows greater depths.

Pin the wadding to the main fabric, with muslin or light cotton underneath, to prevent the wadding tearing on the machine bed. Tack around the edges, across the centres and at 30 cm (12 in) intervals either way to hold the fabrics securely while stitching. Make sure that the tack lines are accurate so that you will be able to follow these with your stitching lines.

If you have chosen a squared design, the bedcover can be cut into four sections, or left in the cut lengths while each section is quilted and then joined together for the final quilting lines. Double machined lines are also much more attractive than a single stitching line. If you choose to hand quilt, a checked design will be easy to follow.

Squares of three complementary fabrics were stitched to a cotton backing, the raw edges concealed under strips of cotton tape and the whole lined in a fourth fabric from the same family.

1

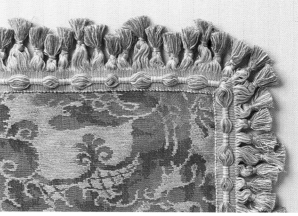

2

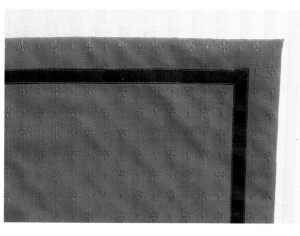

3

4

EDGINGS

1. Quilted bedcovers are best with the addition of a rolled or flat border. If you use the same fabric, add 12 cm (4¾ in) to the measurements and stop the quilting approximately 22 cm (8¾ in) from the outside edges. Stitch a quilting line parallel to the edge, joining up these ends, then add an extra layer of wadding and fold the 22 cm (8¾ in) over to make a 10 cm (4 in) border. Stitch to hold, and cover the raw edge with lining. If you choose a contrast fabric, you will need to cut 22 cm (8¾ in) strips and join them to the quilted cover; pad with wadding and roll under.

2. Bullion or cut fringe edgings may not be practical if you have pets who are allowed into the bedrooms, but otherwise they are perfect for finishing and weighting heavy fabrics such as damasks, brocades, velvets and tapestries.

3. A set-on border using two contrasting fabrics such as these, suggests a finish suitable for a very tailored bed, with the cover fitted over a flat or pleated valance and a collection of tailored pillows in the same fabrics. Choose fabrics which are reluctant to show every crease, interline to give a slightly softer, padded feel and to add weight. Use a good, closely woven braid, tape or gimp and stitch to the main fabric before making up.

4. For a border of 3 cm (1¼ in) cut strips 6 cm (2¼ in) wide. Stitch the border to the bedcover along one long side, stopping 1.5 cm (⅝ in) from the corner. Fold the border strip back on itself to mitre the corner. Start stitching along the bottom edge 1.5 cm (⅝ in) from the corner, and at the same point as the finished first side. Continue with the next corner and to the end.

Cut the outer border strips 9 cm (3½ in) wide. Pin and stitch to the first border in the same way. Press seams towards the inset border. Make up, adding interlining if used. Press the border to the back, folding the corners under to mitre. Herringbone in place and slipstitch the lining over.

FITTED BEDCOVERS

Fitted bedcovers should be lined throughout and may be interlined or quilted on the top. You may like to make decorative pillow covers or shams, or to buy hand-worked linen covers for pillows which sit on top of the bedcover. Or you may prefer to keep pillows hidden using decorative scatter cushions, in which case you will need to add a pillow gusset or attach a pillow flap.

Fitted bedcovers are difficult to use over unwieldy duvets, but work well over sheets and blankets which tuck neatly into the mattress.

MAKING UP

1. Join the cut lengths for the bedcover top as estimated and press the seams flat. Cut and join lining, and interlining, if used. Cut the skirt fabric and lining, join the seams and press. Leave to one side.

2. Lay the bedcover top on to the worktable, right side facing down. Place the interlining, if used, and then the lining over and lock stitch along the seam lines using 5 cm (2 in) stitches to hold the seams together securely. Press both fabrics together and pin around all edges at 10 cm (4 in) intervals. Trim away any excess lining and interlining so that all raw edges line up perfectly.

3. Pin the piping around, 2 cm (¾ in) from the raw edges and stitch close to the piping stitching.

4. Join the skirt lining to the main fabric. Place the skirt along the length of the worktable, wrong side facing down. Place the lining over, right side facing down and pin together along the hemline. Stitch 1.5-2 cm (⅝-¾ in) from the raw edges. If you are using a checked fabric then pin and stitch from the fabric side and follow the line of the checks.

The easiest way to handle a long piece like this, is to work along the length of the worktable, and then to fold the prepared fabric concertina-style, leaving this at the end of the table while you work on the next stage.

5. Press the skirt from the right side, pressing the lining away from the fabric. Turn over and fold the lining up so that 3 cm (1¼ in) of the main fabric is showing. Pin together along the top and trim away excess lining. Press under 2 cm (¾ in) of main fabric and lining at each open end and slipstitch along the fold to neaten.

6. Stitch a double gathering thread through, 1.5 cm and 2 cm (⅝ in and ¾ in) from the raw edges. Divide the length into 10 equal sections and mark each one with a coloured tack.

7. Divide the three sides of the bedcover top into 10 equal sections and mark with coloured tacks. Pin the skirt to the top, matching the relevant tacks. Pull up the gathering thread, one section at a time, and distribute the gathers evenly. Pin along the piping and across, so that the cross pins can be left in place to hold the gathers while stitching. You should have pins at approximately 2 cm (¾ in) intervals for the neatest finish.

8. Neaten the seam with binding. Cut a 10 cm (4 in) strip of main fabric, the width of the cover top. Stitch this strip along the top of the cover, right sides facing together, and as tight to the piping as possible. Press the strip under and in half to enclose the raw edges. Slipstitch to the lining, folding under the ends to neaten.

INTERLINED COVER

If you are using interlining, lock the interlining to the main fabric at step 2 and leave the lining to one side until the skirt has been attached. At step 6, lock stitch the lining to the interlining seams, press all the layers together and pin approximately 10 cm (4 in) from the outer edges, all around. Press the gathered seam and the cover top seam towards the cover top and herringbone to the interlining. Fold the lining under and slip stitch along the stitching line to enclose all raw edges.

PILLOWS

If you want to keep your pillows underneath this style of cover you will need to make some allowance for them. You will either need to add a pillow gusset or a pillow flap, the size of which will depend how many pillows you prefer.

Pillow gusset
Cut the fabric side pieces as shown in Measuring and Estimating, page 10. Stitch the gusset to the cover top and make up as before, following the instructions for the lined or the interlined cover, and cutting these pieces as needed.

Pillow flap
Cut out the fabric, lining and interlining pieces, join any seams and press flat. Place the fabric on to the worktable, right side down, and if interlining is used lock stitch to the seams. Trim in line with the top and 3 cm (1¼ in) in along the other three sides. Press the fabric 3 cm (1¼ in) to the wrong side along the hem and two sides and herringbone stitch to secure. Place the lining over and lock stitch to the seams. Trim away 1 cm (⅜ in) from each of the sides and hem, and slip stitch to cover the raw edges.

Leave on one side, and make up the cover following the instructions above. Attach to the bedcover at step 6.

COMFORTERS

Natural silk and waxed leather thread add strength to fine creamy cotton lawn to complement the luxurious leopard skin bed cushions.

Comforters are extremely practical and useful bedding additions. More compact than duvets, larger than old fashioned eiderdowns, comforters will fold into a cupboard neatly when not needed, or can be rolled up and left at the foot of the bed. Use as the sole bedding over sheets for warmer weather and as extra insulation over sheets and blankets for colder nights. Comforters can be made as two thin layers which might be used separately or fastened together for double insulation.

As with all bedlinen, it is wise to select fabrics and finishes which are easily laundered. If the comforter is to be used often, perhaps doubling as a throw over a sofa bed, or mainly by children and teenagers, then strong washable cotton prints or even a hard-wearing denim needs to be chosen.

Comforters also make ideal covers for day beds, as they are comfortable for sitting on, neat to fit and easy to dress, rolling back to make way for a duvet cover or remaining in place over sheets and blankets for a house guest. As day beds make excellent occasional sofas-come-guest beds, especially in studies, book rooms and sitting rooms, so you can enjoy using elaborate, heavy and decorative covers in damasks, silks or chintzes, as long as the fabrics or fabric combination will allow occasional dry cleaning.

DUVETS

Navy blue demin could be any teenager's choice of bedding. Unusual fastenings add that special finish. Here, large buttonholes stitched with black wool take chunky duffle coat toggles.

Duvets are arguably the most used form of bed covering today. Originating in Scandinavia and designed to combat the extreme cold, their popularity as easy care and versatile bedding has spread worldwide in just two decades, responding in part to our increasingly busy lifestyles. A quick shake and the bed is made: starched and ironed sheets being now a thing of the past and the privilege only of luxury hotels and those of us fortunate enough to have good local laundries.

Originally duvets were filled with down, on the principle that air caught between the fine, fluffy feathers traps body heat, so the covering is to a degree self-regulating and light to sleep under. Channels stitched from top to bottom hold the filling in place, to be shaken to the bottom in warmer weather and distributed throughout the duvet in cold weather. Polyester and feather/fibre or feather/down mixes at all price levels are now available, although there is still nothing to touch a fine down filling, which is so light that the sleeper is unaware of a covering at all.

Designing and making your own, much more attractive duvets covers, could not be simpler. Experiment with fabrics – there are many washable old favourites available such as denim, gingham, fresh stripes and country florals which can be used on their own with striking detail or mixed together. Add contrast borders with buttoned or tied edgings, appliqué a teddy or a boat for a child's cover or pick out the floral motifs from the curtain fabric.

Duvet-covered beds often look uninspiring, as easy-care cotton and polyester covers which fade quickly with washing have largely replaced crisp linen and cotton. Designing and making your own covers will take no more time than choosing and buying ready-made ones and the finished result will be so much more rewarding. Even if you have never stitched anything in your life before, I am confident that duvet covers will not be beyond your reach.

Many fabrics may be used to make duvet covers – of course washability is essential, but you can prolong the life and the times between washing by always using a top sheet under the duvet.

One way to economise when the top fabric is rather expensive, is to use a sheet for the underside and your chosen fabric for the top only. Use washable country and floral prints with checks and stripes or put two similarly coloured but different scaled prints together. Re-vitalise traditional gingham and denim, use them on their own or with more sophisticated fabrics. Traditional French toile de jouy has long been a popular bedroom choice, and is especially lovely combined with simple Normandy striped cottons.

For variety, the top of the duvet cover could be lightly quilted, patchworked, or appliquéd with your own design. Co-ordinate your design with the headboard and valance coverings. Add interest to the design by mixing several colours, such as black, grey and red or French blue and white with a yellow ochre edging.

DECORATIVE DETAILS

How much smarter the most basic green checked fabric and white sheets have become below simply by using two scales of the same check. The large check forms a cheerful border on the duvet, while a narrow cornflower blue border has been added to the edge of the sheet for an effective contrast. Finish the duvet with fun teddy bear buttons, which make ideal fastenings for a child's, or grandchild's bedroom.

Self-fabric ties make a pretty edge for chintzes, stripes or toiles (right).

Buttonholes can be made by hand or with a machine setting: choose fun buttons like these teddies (below). Buttons can be substituted with toggles or leather balls if you use heavy workmanlike fabrics, such as denim, tweed and wool (right).

DESIGN AND MAKE BEDROOM FURNISHINGS

MAKING UP

Take the measurements for your duvet cover from an existing cover or add 2 cm (¾ in) each way to the actual duvet size. You can buy fabrics which are wide enough without seaming but the designs and colours are limited, so plan to join with French or flat seams which will not tear with constant washing. Add 10 cm (4 in) to the length to make plackets for the opening.

I prefer the fastenings to be at the bottom end but they can be put to one side, if you wish. Once you have chosen the style of fastening, add the relevant amount of fabric to your measurements.

No extra allowance will be needed for buttoned or tied fastenings. For straightforward fastenings (buttons or poppers) the top will fold under in three to make a strong edge for the top fastener or buttonhole and the bottom will fold in half to make a placket to hold the buttons or bottom fastener. For ties, the 10 cm (4 in) allowance will need to be cut away, the ties inserted and the raw edges folded under and slipstitched to enclose the seams. Added borders will need double the width of the finished border, plus seam allowances: button holes, eyelets or poppers will fix into the border.

Ties made in the same fabric as the cover provide an effective and practical fastening (left, centre). Instead of stitching the ties to the cover, use an eyelet kit and thread the ties through these for a really neat and stylish finish (left, bottom).

FOOT FLAP WITHOUT FASTENING

To keep a duvet in place, I often insert a foot flap – a strip of fabric set into the underside which can be tucked into the mattress to prevent feet escaping.

Make up a strip of fabric 50 cm (20 in) narrower than the duvet × 50 cm (20 in), turning the seams under on the bottom and sides. Allow 10 cm (4 in) extra length to the underside of the cover and cut across the width 35 cm (13¾ in) from the end. Stitch the flap to the main piece, right sides together and neaten the seam. Pin the 35 cm (13¾ in) piece back on, setting the flap seam 6 cm (2¾ in) down. Stitch together on either side of the flap. Fold the 8 cm (3¾ in) under twice and stitch across. Neaten the seams to the side of the flap.

Join the duvet top and bottom together around all four sides. Insert the duvet through the foot flap opening.

FOOT FLAP WITH FASTENING

If you want to add a flap but have designed a bottom fastening, make up the flap as before, allow only 4 cm (1½ in) extra to the length, cut away 27 cm (10¾ in) from the end and re-join to the main piece with the foot flap inserted between. Join the top and sides together and continue with your chosen fastening.

SHEETS

Falling leaves make wonderfully free and varied shapes to appliqué randomly, echoing the restful balance of natural silk, wool and embroidery with jute, fine and unbleached linens.

After many years of easy-care cotton and polyester/cotton mixes being the sole option easily available, the consumer has demanded a revival of pure cotton and linen bed sheets and pillowcases. There is nothing quite like the pleasure of fresh and fragrant smelling, laundered and lightly starched sheets as, work weary, one climbs into a newly changed bed.

Fine linen sheets are the elite and consequently very expensive to buy and often hard to locate. Heavy duty, tightly woven cotton is always a good substitute – keep looking in antique linen markets to find sheets and pillowcases in good condition and search out mail order companies offering commercial-quality width fabrics from which to make your own. Sometimes you will be fortunate enough to buy best quality linen sheeting as an end of roll or end of line. This type of sheeting is usually only available in white, but this hardly matters as whites always look good and are so accommodating to launder. Any washable fabrics are suitable, although you really do need wide width fabrics as seams can be very uncomfortable to lie on.

PILLOWS

Pillow shams are purely decorative covers which slip over the pillow, dressing the bed by day and one or more removed at night to reveal the plainer, functional covers beneath

I remember a discussion at school which concluded that sleeping on pillows was bad for the spine and only for 'softies'! I really do not know the medical viewpoint – I just know that, if given the choice, I would always rather lay my head on plump, down-filled pillows than a hard mattress. In any case, the bed can hardly be dressed without pillows and cushions, whether they are functional or purely decorative.

The most luxurious and dreamy filling for pillows is the very best down, at present from Hungary or China. In fact, these pillows are so light and soft that they are most effective when used on top of one with a more substantial filling. Down and feather mixes are a less expensive but perfectly adequate option, a higher percentage of down makes a softer pillow. Fibre fillings should only be chosen for those who are highly allergic to feathers as they do not last long and soon become flat, mis-shapen and uncomfortable.

While there are many styles, patterns and colours of pillowcases available 'off the peg', you will pay a great deal for well-made, decorative pillowcases. And buying someone else's design is not nearly as much fun as designing and making your own.

The only time when I would not hesitate to buy pillowcases is when I am designing a bed which needs white linen. A pile of freshly starched, Oxford-style pillows with hand-stitched drawn thread edgings looks wonderful, clean and elegant. If you prefer a country look there are well made, beautifully hand-embroidered white cotton cases from Portugal, Madeira and the Far East, to mix with antique cushions, sheets and nightdress cases.

If you are in rather a hurry, you could buy the plainest white cases which you can then decorate without spending much time at all. Use rows of ribbons and braids: stitch along the sides or all around an Oxford edge or bind the edges with a plain contrast, polka dots and checks, tartans and plaids.

HOUSEWIFE STYLE

1. Measure the width and height of your pillow, add 1.5 cm (⅝ in) all around for seam allowances and an extra 8 cm (3¼ in) to the back width and 20 cm (8 in) to the front. It is usual to put the opening on the right hand side. Cut out two pieces.

2. Place the smaller piece on to the worktable, right side down. Turn the 8 cm (3¼ in) to the back. Fold under to make 4 cm (1⅝ in) and machine stitch along the fold line. Repeat with the front piece, using 5 cm (2 in) of the allowance.

3. Place the front piece on to the table, right side facing up. Place the back piece over so that right sides are facing, and pin around three sides. Fold the flap over, pin to the other two sides along the top and bottom edges and stitch.

OXFORD STYLE

1. Measure the size of your pillow and add 2 cm (¾ in) seam allowances. Add the depth of the border – approximately 6 cm (2¼ in) – to each side. So a 70 × 50 cm (28 × 20 in) pillow will need to have a front piece 86 × 66 cm (34 × 26 in). The back will need to be cut as two pieces to make an opening for the pillow. Allow 14 cm (5½ in) extra to the opening side and 24 cm (9½ in) to the main back piece. (One piece 66 × 106 cm/26 × 41½ in and one piece 66 × 26 cm/26 × 10 in.) Cut out three pieces.

2. Make 2 cm (¾ in) double turnings along the opening edges of both back pieces. Place the pillow front on to the table, right side facing up. Place the main back piece over, matching up the three raw edges, and fold the opening edge back 20 cm (8 in). Place the smaller piece over, matching the raw edges, and overlapping the flap by 10 cm (4 in). Pin to secure. Stitch all around, neaten the seams and turn out. Press flat.

3. Measure a 6 cm (2¼ in) border inside the outer edge all around. Stitch along this line. Add narrow ribbon, braid or use a decorative stitch for individual detail.

Scalloped-edged Oxford

All Oxford-style pillow covers are made as above. For a scalloped edge, allow more depth for the border, and shape the edge using a template made by drawing around a wine glass or saucer. Make piping and stitch all around, following the shaped edge closely. Make up following the instructions above from step 2.

MIXING PILLOWS

Navy blue and white are always elegant and can be employed for the most formal bedrooms. Plain colours and stripes are rewarding for the way in which they can always be used together to different effect. The striped bed curtains are bordered in the same dark blue as the main pillow cover and the other two cushions are piped in the stripe, on the cross and on the straight. A toile de jouy bedcover and the frilled pillow add an air of informality, the white lifting the deep blue from the dark wood bed head. The white pillow cover is designed to be used as it is easily laundered; the more formal piped, scalloped-edged Oxford cushion and the bordered scatter cushion are more for effect, to be put to one side when the bed is in use.

FRILLED PILLOW COVERS

Any fabric can be frilled as long as the amount of fullness and the depth of frill are adjusted to suit each situation – a fine lawn will need three times fullness for body, but will flop if more than 8 cm (3¼ in) deep. In some cases a very floppy frill can be attractive; make a small template if you are at all unsure. Heavier fabrics such as velvet and damasks need less than double fullness and will be rather stiff if too short. Make up to between 8 cm (3¼ in) and 12 cm (4¾ in).

It is often the unexpected element that makes a design scheme work, and the lilac gingham is certainly a surprise with the subdued tones of a dog's tooth check bedcover and the rich browns and reds of the hand-printed cotton sheet and pillow cover.

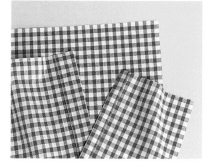

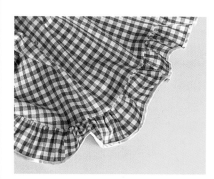

1. Measure your pillow and add 2 cm (¾ in) for seam allowances. Cut the front piece to these measurements. Add 8 cm (3¼ in) to the width and cut one back piece. Cut another piece the depth of the front piece and 14 cm (5½ in) wide. Use the 8 cm (3¼ in) piece to make a double turning on the opening side of the main back piece and 2 cm (¾ in) double turnings on the opening side of the smaller piece.

2. Cut widths of fabric to make the frill, allowing 4 cm (1½ in) for turnings and join with flat seams to make a loop. Make a 1 cm (⅜ in) double turning along the outside edge and stitch down, close to the fold line. Stitch a gathering thread 2 cm (¾ in) from the opposite raw edge. Divide the whole into 10 equal sections and mark with a coloured tacks.

3. Measure all around the pillow front and mark into 10 equal sections and mark with coloured tacks. Pipe around the edge. Pin the frill to the pillow front, matching the coloured tacks. Pull up the threads within each section and distribute the gathers evenly. Pin at approximately 2 cm (¾ in) intervals. Keep the raw edges lined up all the time so that the frill stays an even width.

4. Pin the larger back piece to the front, right sides together, along the three raw sides. Pin the smaller piece over, again matching the raw edges. Stitch all around, covering the frill stitching line. Neaten the seam, turn the pillowcase out and press.

Finish the frill with bound edges, stitching tape to the outer edges of the frill before gathering up.

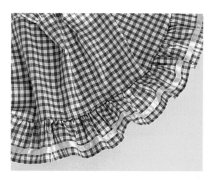

Ribbons or braids can be stitched parallel to the outer edge before gathering up.

Double frills need to be made from fabrics of the same content and structure to avoid any possible laundering problems.

PILLOW SHAMS

Pillow shams are decorative covers for pillows, open at one end and designed to be fitted easily over pillows with plain covers in the morning and removed at night.

Antique Victorian lace is the perfect decorative finish for the country bed, complementing crisp linens, cheerful ginghams and floral prints.

Make the pillowsham about 10 cm (4 in) longer than the pillow, adding frilled or lace ends which flop down to hide the pillow inside.

There are several benefits to making pillow shams rather than elaborate pillowcases. To begin with, very complex decoration and delicate fabrics can be used without the need for constant washing and pressing to keep the covers looking fresh. Also, different pillow shams made for each bedroom allow the household linen to be a single plain colour, probably white.

BED CUSHIONS

Scatter cushions made to decorate the bed do not have to stand up to the same wear and tear as those in family rooms, so more elaborate detail and delicate fabrics can be employed. Silk organza, fine white linen, satin ribbons and silky cotton damasks are invitingly soft and elegant. Collect antique lace cotton covers to mix with newly made ones. Nightdress cases can be converted to make lovely cushion covers; add buttons and loops to fasten.

DAY BEDS AND BOLSTERS

Toile de jouy print in an original colourway is made up with a simple woven stripe from unbleached cotton. Tiny fabric-covered buttons and calico tape close the covers along each side.

Antique day beds are one of the most versatile pieces of furniture you can buy. Suitable for use in bedrooms, sitting rooms, drawing rooms and even in hallways and on landings, day beds adapt easily to family seating, changing immediately to accommodate a house guest as needed. Look out for solid, masculine pine or mahogany beds for heavier use and delicate carved and painted styles for drawing rooms and bedrooms. The fabrics and trimmings which can be used to furnish day beds have no limits. Heavy damasks in rich colours with copious braiding and tassels would do credit to those in Versailles. The same bed dressed with white linen, floaty muslin drapes with a primitive patchworked bedcover would not look out of place on a Greek Island.

Try toiles with self-coloured stripes for an early country style, an abundance of spring and summer flowers printed on glazed chintzes for a country house look, richly coloured paisley prints tasselled and mixed with tapestries and kelims for an eastern feel, tartans and wools for the Scottish shooting lodge atmosphere – the list is virtually endless.

Bolsters at each end reflect the traditional upholstery designs and, if made to fit along the length will help to hold the back cushions. Fill the back with deep boxed cushions and piles of scatter cushions for comfortable seating.

BOLSTERS

Bolsters are the cylindrical cushions which traditionally rested along the width of the bed and were used as we now use pillows. In particular, they are wonderful decorative and practical additions to day beds. Bolster fillings should always have a high proportion of down so that the bolster is light enough to handle easily, and soft enough to be really comfortable.

Bolster covers are very straightforward to make, at their simplest a cylinder needing one seam and two hems. These bolsters are made following the most basic method with six different tied ends.

Measure the circumference of the bolster and add 4 cm (1½ in) for the seam allowance. Measure the length of the bolster from halfway across each end and add 8 cm (3 in) for hems. These measurements form the basic fabric rectangle needed to cover the pad and any other finishes should be added to this measurement.

1. This 'flower' end was created with two strips of fabric in a contrast colour. Stitch the strips to either end, right sides together. Stitch a French seam along the length. Fold the end pieces in half, press the raw edges under and slip stitch to the seam line. Fill the bolster and tie the ends very tightly with ribbon or rouleau ties.

2. Here, the cover was made in two halves, adding 30 cm (12 in) to each end of the basic length.

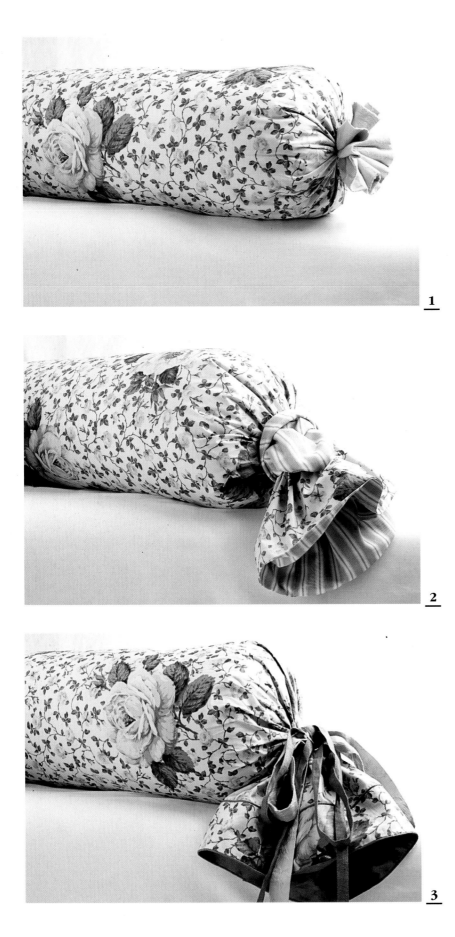

Cut two pieces of main fabric and four pieces of contrast (yellow) fabric 35 (13½ in). Pin and stitch the four pieces of yellow to the four ends of the bolster pieces. Turn right sides out and join the two bolster pieces together with French seams. Neaten lining edges, fill the bolster and tie the ends.

3. This bolster cover is simply knotted and the end 'belled' out. Make the cover longer on each side than the basic pattern and line ends with a complementary fabric. Join the length with a flat fell or French seam. Neaten lining edges, fill the cover and tie ends into a loose knot.

4. Make the bolster cover 55 cm (22 in) longer each side than the basic pattern. Cut extra strips of main fabric to make a border at each end and contrast fabric for linings. Pipe around the two short ends of the bolster. Stitch the border strip to the same piping line. Pipe around this border. Stitch the lining piece to this stitching line. Using a flat fell seam, join the length of the bolster. Neaten lining edges, press and fold to the inside. Fill the cover and tie each end in a loose knot.

5. Picking up a secondary colour and using it for the piping adds an effective detail.

6. This cover is made 35 cm (14 in) longer at each end than the basic pattern. Join the length and hem in the usual way. Fill the bolster and tie with four rouleau ties made from a dark green fabric. Fan out the end to look like an open flower.

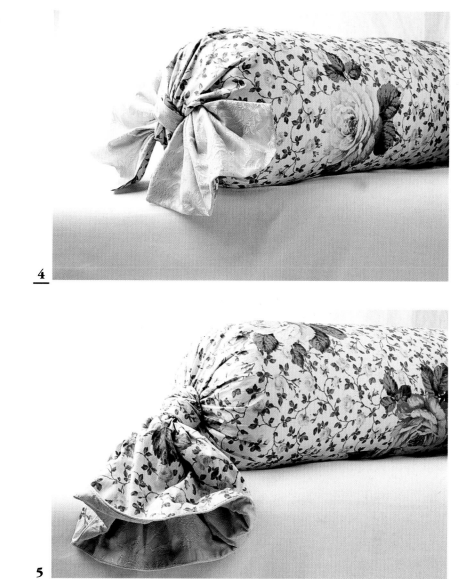

4

5

6

BED
CURTAINS

Ethereal and romantic, this bed dressing has been created with yards of muslin, antique cotton bed linen and silks in creams and whites.

Beds were originally curtained with heavy tapestries, lengths of wool, silk brocade, or heavy cotton to keep the bitter cold air out as lack of window coverings and inadequate heating allowed the wind to whistle around ancient castles and manor houses.

In humbler abodes, floor rugs were hung over doors and windows at night to keep out the cold. Thankfully, bed curtains are no longer necessary for warmth but are often desirable for atmosphere.

Original or reproduction copies of early, solid wooden four poster beds look undressed without some form of curtaining as do the tall metal frames fashionable at the moment. During the last century particularly, some beds were made as half testers: that is with a frame to hold curtains which fitted the width of the bed head but which projected just 60-70 cm (24-28 in). Bed curtains hang behind the bed and to either side; the side curtains drape back against the wall. Sometimes a fabric pelmet was fitted between the curtains and the tester frame.

Coronas are fitted either centrally above the bed from the ceiling, or on to the back wall, central to the width of the bed. Four curtains fall from a centre corona, draping out to each corner, and two curtains form a wall corona, draping from the front and back to either side of the bed head.

UNLINED BED CURTAINS

Unlined curtains are the easiest to make and extremely effective when plenty of fabric is used to create softness and body. Suitable fabrics are muslin, fine linen, tana lawn, organdie, organza, natural or bleached calico, lightweight silks, ticking and simple stripes. The fabric should look as good from the inside as the outside. Headings need to be finished so that both sides can be appreciated.

MAKING UP

To make four curtains, one for each corner which will pull to close, use at least two widths of fabric for each curtain and three to four widths for sheer fabrics.

1. Cut and join lengths, allowing 8 cm (3¼ in) turnings for the heading and 4 cm (1½ in) for the hem. Lightweight curtains should be overlong, and don't forget to allow the draping allowance if the curtains are to be tied up. Use flat seams and press thoroughly.

2. Working with one curtain at a time, press 4 cm (1½ in) to the wrong side of each side and hem. Press in half and fold under to make 2 cm (¾ in) turnings. Mitre the bottom corners, stitch with a decorative machine stitch or slip stitch by hand along the fold; press.

3. Place the curtain on to the worktable and press flat. Measure from the hem to the heading and mark the overall drop. Mark 8 cm (3¼ in) above this line and trim away any excess. Press the 8 cm (3¼ in) allowance to the wrong side. Press in half to make a 4 cm (1⅝ in) turning. Pin all along.

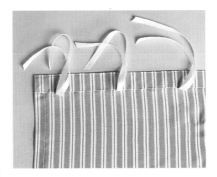

4. For a simple heading, cut ribbons or tapes to the required length. Fold in half and pin under the fold line at regular intervals the length of the heading. Stitch close to the fold line, carefully double stitching over the ribbons or tapes to secure and stitch another row 5 mm (¼ in) from the overall drop line.

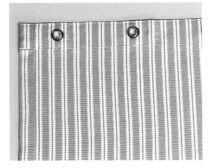

5. If you are using eyelets, make holes and fit the eyelets at regular intervals along the top once all the stitching is complete.

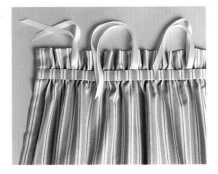

6. To disguise the back of the gathering tape, cut a band of main fabric, fold under the raw edges and slip stitch in place.

HEADINGS

If the curtains are to hang from a metal rail they will need to look as good inside as outside.

Insert a piece of 5 cm (2 in) buckram between the interlining and the inner curtain. Herringbone to the interlining. Fold both fabrics in and slip stitch together to match the sides.

If the curtains are being fitted beneath a pelmet or behind a corona, the hooks will be fitted from the front, as the inside of the bed hangings will be seen. Either gather by hand or use bought heading tapes. Fold both fabrics to the front and stitch whichever heading tape you choose to use, approximately 2 cm (¾ in) from the top. Pull up threads or gather by hand.

Unlined curtains made from beige and white ticking are fastened to the metal frame with ties made from curtain heading tape. Overlong curtains bunch into extravagant drapes at each corner.

CANOPIES

Canopies need not be formal in the way that coronas and four poster beds are, and they need not be purely decorative. In many countries mosquito nets are an essential part of the bed drapes, and it is fun to incorporate them into more decorative bed hangings. You can either buy ready-made hoops with netting attached or make your own using metres (yards) of fine cotton or cotton and polyester netting. For safety, choose fabrics which are flame retardant.

For one island bedroom we stitched metres of fine cotton netting together to make a huge 'box' large enough to cover the bed completely. The centre and four corners had self ties stitched into the seams, then fitted to the ceiling with huge brass hooks. We untied four jute tasselled tiebacks and slipped them through the same corner hooks, to hold the netting out of the way during the day time.

For another bedroom, we made four single curtains which threaded on to a metal hoop fitted over the centre of the bed. The hoop was suspended on a chain which finished approximately 30 cm (12 in) below the ceiling. Four unlined bed curtains were knotted together above the hoop, draped back to each corner and tied. Each morning the net curtains are just twisted once around each of the bed curtains and dropped down at night to keep out unwanted bugs. These net curtains do need to be at least double fullness so that the sides meet and stay closed.

Summer canopies always look stunning with stripes from the narrowest ticking to the widest tent or sailing canvas. Choose fabrics which are washable and presentable, even if they crease. I always send unknown and stiff fabrics to the laundry, from where they return beautifully soft (make sure you ask them not to add starch) and with the shrinkage excess taken out.

One of the main principles of good design is that rooms should be changeable – so a bed canopy or curtains hanging for the winter months can transform easily to a fresher, brighter summer version. I like to choose sheer white linen curtains in the summer months which make way for heavily interlined weaves and prints in the winter.

Tropical prints in strong colour combinations also look wonderful for summer bed canopies, as do antique sheets, white or unbleached muslin, calico, freshly coloured chintzes, strong leafy prints and plain or printed Indian cotton panels and bedcovers. Hold curtains with tiebacks, cord loops, lengths of cord, canvas or leather strips, metal holdbacks or have small pillars or short bedposts made to drape the canopy curtains over.

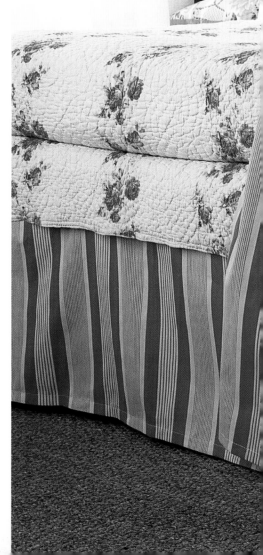

A beautiful antique hand-quilted Welsh bedcover provided the inspiration for this summer bedroom. The pink and white striped bed curtains and padded bed head cover are made from mattress ticking.

HALF TESTER CURTAINS

Follow the instructions for unlined, lined or interlined bed curtains, measuring the cuts as shown on pages 54, 56 and 57. If the half tester is made as a substantial frame, then the headings will be unseen from the front, so you can use bought heading tape to gather or pleat. If the frame is a metal or wooden pole, then the curtains will either hook into rings or tie around the poles with self ties, ribbons or fabric tabs, as the heading will be seen from both front and back. In this case, either hand gather, set heading tape between the inner and outer curtains, or stitch tape to the inside and make a fabric strip which will cover the tape when pulled up, and slip stitch top and bottom, holding the gathers with tiny stitches.

PELMETS

Make a template to design your pelmet shape and pin to the wood frame when you are satisfied with the size and shape. Cut the front and back fabrics and interlining. Allow two-and-a-half to three times fullness for both tester and corona pelmets and cut pieces for the outer and inner fabrics and interlining. Join, press seams and lock stitch together as for curtains. Treat the hem in the same way as the sides of the curtains, and bring the inner fabric right to the folded edge. Slip stitch and add your chosen trimming. If you are binding the edge, follow the curtain binding instructions.

The pelmet will fit to the front of the wooden board so make gathered or pinch pleated headings with the tape stitched on the inside. Stitch touch and close tape on to the pulled up heading and fit to the opposite side around the tester or corona.

Twist double ropes and stitch to cover the stitching lines.

SUN RAY PLEATING

Unless the half tester or corona is a wood or metal frame, the inside will need to be covered. The most attractive way is to pleat the fabric in a sun ray design.

1. Mark the centre of the corona at the front and back. Cut three fabric widths of fabric so that the length is 50 per cent longer than the widest angle of the corona.

2. Starting at the centre, place one piece of the fabric right side up, so that it overlaps the centre line by 2 cm (¾ in). Fold the fabric so that the first pleat is towards the middle line and aligns with the centre line.

3. Continue to fold the fabric, measuring the fold sizes carefully so that they are all equal on the outside edge. These pleats can be between 1.5 cm (⅝ in) and 3 cm (1¼ in) apart, based on personal preference and the amount of fabric available.

4. Keep the straight of grain correct, and pile the folds over each other on the inside edge. Only finger press the pleats, if the pleats are pressed too flat the finish will have no life or body. If the fabric gets too thick at the centre, cut away from underneath to trim the bulk, first making sure that each piece is secured at another point.

5. Staple underneath each pleat at the back, and staple each pleat on to the front of the corona around the shaping. The pleats will automatically form a semi-circle. Make a choux rosette or cover a large button to finish off the centre and cover the raw edges.

A favourite chintz in soft greens, greys and white, is lined with a tiny trefoil motif in aqua blue. The valance shows how well the two fabrics work together.

CURTAIN DETAILS

Decorative finishes such as sashes and bows can make the most of even the simplest fabrics. Soft fluid fabrics which drape and tie easily make full, floppy bows. Or set firmer bows to a rigid, formal shape by steeping in starch.

MAKING A SASH

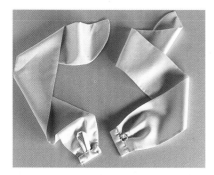

To establish the length of the sash, drape a length of scrap fabric around your curtain, trim to size, tie a bow or knot to the front or side of the curtain, pin in position and mark where the rings should be stitched to fit the tieback hook.

Cut fabric the length and twice the width of your template, fold in half with right sides together and stitch from each end to the centre, leaving a 12 cm (4¾ in) gap. Trim the seams back to 5 mm (¼ in), turn through, press and slip stitch the opening. Cut this length into two as shown, turn under the raw edges and pleat the sash ends to approximately 3 cm (1¼ in). Stitch to neaten and stitch a ring just inside one end and a fabric loop in the other. Fit on to the hook and tie into a bow or knot. Stitch so that the bow or knot cannot easily be undone.

MAKING A BOW

To make this bow, cut two pieces of fabric 45 × 12 cm (18 × 4¾ in) and piping to go all round. Stitch the piping to the right side of one piece, very close to the piping stitching line. Place the other piece of fabric over the top, pin carefully in place and stitch from the first side, keeping your stitching line just inside the last one. Leave a 12 cm (4¾ in) gap in the middle. Trim the seams to 5 mm (¼ in) and turn right side out. Pull the corners out with a pin and press along the seam line. Slip stitch the gap, pin the bow to the worktable and tie. Stitch the bow in position so that no one can come along and untie your beautiful creation.

MAKING A ROSE

Use different lengths and widths of fabric for different sized roses and buds. For this rose, cut one piece of fabric 1 m (1 yd) long, making it 14 cm (5½ in) at one end and 10 cm (4 in) at the other. Fold in half lengthwise and run a hand-stitched gathering thread 1.5 cm (⅝ in) in from the raw edges. Pull up to 50 cm (20 in) and, starting at the narrow end, roll up to make the rose, keeping the raw edges tight together. Stitch through all layers to hold the shape, cut a small square of fabric and stitch to the back to cover the frayed ends.

TIES

Simple ties also make very effective tiebacks. Tie a piece of tape or an offcut of fabric around your curtain to determine the length and width of the tie and follow the making up instructions on page 8.

Checked and striped fabrics for ties can be bought quite inexpensively and are most effective when used cut on the cross or in complementary colours and different weaves to the main fabrics.

ROULEAUX

To make a rouleau measuring 45 × 6 cm (18 × 2¼ in) cut a strip of fabric 50 × 14 cm (20 × 5½ in) and a piece of polyester wadding 50 × 70 cm (20 × 28 in). Roll up the wadding and loosely herringbone. Press under 1.5 cm (⅝ in) along one length. Fold this strip over the wadding roll, pin the folded edge over the raw edge and slip stitch. Cut two small pieces to stitch over the ends, with a ring at one end and a fabric loop at the other.

Large bows and sashes for feminine bedrooms (left) can be made simply and quickly or in much more detail with contrast linings, pipings and ribbons.

HEADBOARD COVERS

Vibrant golds and reds, depicting the story of the discovery of America, make an unusual choice for bedroom furnishings, responding to the golden colours of the antique pine bed head.

Slip covers can be made to fit over any headboard, whether cane, wood, or upholstered. Simple lined covers can tie or button over a plain headboard to add warmth to the room, to pick up a particular fabric or colour within the overall decoration, or just to create a little more comfort when you are sitting up in bed. Slip covers can also be easily padded or quilted for extra body and comfort.

You might want an extra cover which is washable – this is especially useful for a guest bedroom. Or you might have a lovely upholstered headboard which you want to protect. I often also make a slip cover in matching fabric to combine comfort with washability. A slip cover can change the style completely or disguise an ugly fabric beneath, such as covering a velvet buttoned headboard with a chintz slip cover. It will also give you the opportunity to use an upholstered velvet cover with your winter furnishings and change to summery chintzes for the warmer months.

If possible, I prefer to make slip covers double sided, but if you are using an expensive fabric or have a limited amount to use, then just border the back so that the lining is not visible. Finish with contrast or self piping, cords or rope edgings in mixed colours or a strong contrast. Close with ties, buttons, tabs, ribbons or braids for practical decoration.

SLIP COVER DESIGNS

Design your own slip cover to suit whatever style of bed or bedroom you have to work with. With a little imagination and following the basic instructions given, you can adapt these ideas to design your own slip cover.

Quilting the front piece will help if your headboard is a little flat. If you are covering a headboard which is already padded and buttoned, choose a quilted fabric or quilt your own to prevent the fabric following the contours and dipping into the buttoned recesses.

As long as the basic shape is good, any unfashionable wooden headboard can be given a new lease of life with a slip cover. Firstly, re-upholster the wooden board with fire retardant foam and calico to give you a soft and comfortable back to sit against.

If you wish to make a new bed head, first cut a paper template and pin to the wall behind the bed to check the shape. Consider the pictures you might want to hang above, whether you want to have a canopy and what shape this will be, how many pillows you will need and how high.

Piping the edge of a bed head cover helps to identify the line, especially if the shape is quite intricate as the one shown above. This board was designed to reflect the cottage-style bed legs and the lovely draped canopy. Brown gingham was an unusual choice, and perhaps such a traditional fabric as to be often overlooked, but proving once again that even the simplest fabric can be made to look wonderful with the right design and detailed finishes. Piping should be bold enough to define the edge but not so strong as to overpower. A deep tone picked up from the main fabric can give definition to a floral or all over print.

Your bed head should finish on the divan, below the mattress and be approximately 3 cm (1¼ in) wider than the width of the bed. Use foam approximately 4 cm (1½ in) deep and position the foam so that it starts at the top of the mattress; any lower and it will not fit correctly but instead will push the mattress forwards.

Cut the foam to shape and glue to the wood with a PVA glue. Staple all around approximately 3 mm (⅛ in) from the edge of the foam, making a neat rounded edge. Stretch calico over the front, staple to the back of the board and make a back lining also with calico. Pull the calico tight for wrinkle-free corners.

Tied sides look very attractive (below), especially when made from a contrast fabric, ribbon or a check or striped fabric cut on the cross. But ties do not always need to be functional: make up a bordered headboard and stitch purely decorative ties or ribbons opposite each other into the piping seams. Tie in generous floppy bows or small, neat ties.

This cover (above) consists only of two pieces of lined fabric, one for the front and one for the back, shaped exactly as the wooden board, lined and with eyelets inset at intervals all around the top. Self ties thread though from front to back and tie in bold loops. Unlike the picture on the right, these ties are essential to hold the cover in place. Buttons and tabs, button-holes and toggles or button-holes and cufflinks could have been used instead for an individual touch.

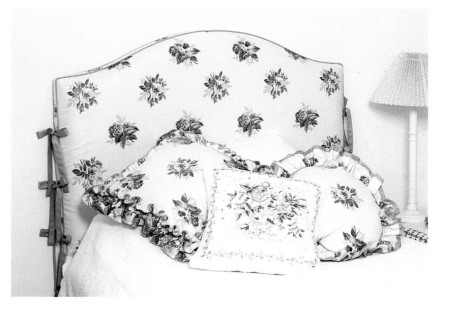

To add some interest to an all white scheme, I used a picot edging in cream instead of piping (right). A flap in matching white damask edged with the same creamy picot lace is fastened down with pearl buttons. Cushions and pillows in cream and white silks, cottons and organdies emphasise the 'elegant romantic' style.

HEADBOARD COVERS

BEDROOM TABLES

A corner dressing table doubles up as a bedside table in a small bedroom. A separate top with valance front can be removed for washing.

Dressing tables need to be positioned wherever possible to make the best advantage of natural daylight. For this reason, it is often inadvisable to use antique pieces of furniture or any good wood which might bleach and warp in strong sunlight, or might be affected by chemicals or acids spilling from toiletries. Fabric-covered dressing tables are ideal, especially if the fabric top can be washed easily. Skirts should also be easily removable for cleaning in case of spills.

Kidney-shaped dressing tables with shelved doors and consequent storage are sometimes available from auctions and can be transformed with new curtains. An old table or desk can be re-employed as a dressing table – always choose a solid piece of furniture, but cut a new top which is at least 5 cm (2 in) larger all around, to allow the curtains to hang straight. Fit a track to the underside to take the skirt.

If you have room in front of a window, a spare corner in your bedroom or enough space next to the bed, consider a fabric-covered display table to hold an extra lamp, picture frames for family photos, books and other objects.

This exuberant floral design, hand-printed in France, needs little extra decoration – the cream lace edging is just enough to lift the hand gathered skirt heading.

Scalloped hems trimmed in a pretty picot lace edge the two unlined fabrics which are then gathered together, finished with hand stitched butterfly edging and the prettiest piped bow.

Corner dressing tables are a design solution which I have often employed, especially in a small room where space is at a premium or wall space is limited.

As walls are rarely at right angles, make a template to fit exactly between the two walls, check that the front shape allows for a stool or chair. Plan the top to be large enough to accommodate an adequate mirror, one or two lights, trays to hold hair slides, brushes and toiletries.

Test other tables in the house to find the perfect knee height. Cut two shelves and fit with large angle brackets to each wall. Make the lower shelf 5 cm (2 in) shallower to allow more knee room and approximately 20 cm (8 in) lower than the table top. Cover the top with interlining and curtain lining stapled securely to the underside. Cover the underside of the top and the lower shelf with fabric. Stick or tack braid to the shelf fronts.

DESIGN AND MAKE BEDROOM FURNISHINGS

A separate top with attached valance can be removed easily for cleaning. Different scale quilting on the top and the valance add charm to the simple country check.

Any free-standing dressing table whether rectangular, oval or kidney shaped can be covered with fabric skirts and tops. Two methods to cover these tables are shown and described. The first, as shown left, has fabric upholstered to the top and curtains which do not pull but fit to the front of the table top. A decorative heading will be needed, but needs to be kept fairly simple for everyday use to prevent soiling. These curtains will lift up to access storage but will be unsuitable if you want to keep everyday products on the shelves below.

If you want the skirts to pull, fit a track to the underside of the table top, following the shape and hang the skirt curtains to them. The top will need a straight, pleated or gathered valance to cover the track.

Almost any fabric can be chosen to cover dressing tables, but obviously heavier weight fabrics will not gather as fully as organdie or muslin. Washable fabrics are useful to have, but not essential. Cotton canvas, bold stripes and geometric prints or weaves can be used for a less feminine approach. Often several layers will work together – such as spotted muslin over organdie, or a pastel coloured chintz, several layers of voile in toning colours.

MAKING THE SKIRT

Measure the length needed for the skirt, whether from the underside of the table or just above the table top. Allow three times fullness for lightweight fabrics and less for stiffer weaves. Skirts should be lined, but will be clumsy if interlined with anything other than the finest domette. Make up the 'curtains' following the instructions on page 56, gather the heading by hand if it shows, but use bought tape for under-curtains. If you are using more than one layer, line the under-curtain and leave the top layers free. Join the layers together with the heading.

MAKING THE TOP

Cut the top fabric to the size of the table top plus 3 cm (1¼ in) all around for turnings. Cut lining and interlining or polyester wadding. Place the lining, wadding and fabric on to the worktable and tack together around the outside and in 10 cm (4 in) squares. Mark the quilting lines and stitch along them, always stitching from the same direction.

Pipe all around using 2 cm (¾ in) seam allowance. Cut strips of fabric 10 cm (4 in) wide and stitch to the two wall sides. Fold these in half and slip stitch to enclose the seam.

Cut the valance to fit around the front. Cut a template to make the scalloped edge using paper and a wine glass or saucer. The scallops should fit exactly into the space. Quilt as before. Pipe around the scalloped edge. Pin to the lining and stitch together, following the scallops closely. Stitch the top of the valance to the top cover and neaten the seam. Fit on to the table top – slip the flaps down between the top and the wall to hold, but use double-sided tape to keep in place if necessary.

TABLECLOTHS

Large display tables are lovely to have in bedrooms to keep lamps, pictures, books, fabric boxes, flowers and ornaments. If you don't have the floor space to fully justify a large table and elaborate cloth, combine display and bedside table with a spare corner. Make the table top as wide as possible, but a minimum of 80 cm (32 in).

The undercloth will stay in place all year round. In the winter it is covered with an antique paisley shawl and in the summer this pretty chintz square is thrown over to complement the summer bed drapes and cover.

MAKING UP

Use boxes and paper circles to determine the height and diameter which best suits the space and the scale of the other furnishings in the room, and either find a junk table or construct a simple one from board.

Measure the diameter and the straight drop to the floor. Add 2–3 cm (¾–1¼ in) for the cloth drape. For example, a table 80 cm high × 100 cm (32 × 39 in) will need a cloth 265 cm (104 in) in diameter. Add seam allowances and cut 271 cm (106½ in). As fabric is usually available in a 135 cm (54 in) width you will need two cuts, each 270 cm (106 in) in length.

1. Cut and join the fabric, keeping a whole width in the centre and a half width on either side. Cut lining and interlining to match, join seams and press flat.

2. Fold the lining into four. Place a metre ruler (yardstick) at the centre fold and mark the radius from one side to the other at 3–5 cm (1¼–2 in) intervals. Join the marks to make a quarter circle. Cut around this line. Re-fold to check that each quarter is the same.

Tones of blue and white meet in a perfect combination with strong blues, bright white and a crisp stripe. The toile de jouy bedcover depicts the scenes surrounding the first hot air balloon flight held in 1783.

3. Place the cloth fabric on to the worktable, right side facing down with the lining over the top. Pin securely and press both fabrics flat. Cut around the lining. Remove the lining and place the interlining over. Lock stitch the interlining to the cloth at each seam and three times across the centre width, following the instructions on page 6. Trim the interlining away 3 cm (1¼ in) inside the fabric circle and herringbone to secure in place.

4. Fold the tablecloth fabric over 3 cm (1¼ in) and herringbone to the interlining. Place the lining over and lock stitch to the interlining. Turn under 2 cm (¾ in) of the lining all around the edge. Pin at 3–5 cm (1¼–2 in) intervals to secure and ease any puckers. Slip stitch to finish.

5. Bind with a contrast fabric or stitch fringe braid to the hemline.

GLOSSARY

FIBRES

Acrylic Manmade from petrol, often mixed with more expensive fibres to keep the cost down. Not hardwearing, but useful for permanent pleating.

Cotton A natural fibre, cotton is very versatile, woven, knitted and mixed with other fibres. Used for any soft furnishings according to weight. It will lose strength in direct sunlight, so protect. Soft, strong, easy to launder, washable if pre-shrunk.

Linen Fibres found inside the stalks of the flax plant are woven to make linen cloth in almost any weight. Distinctive slub weave from very fine linen for under-curtains and sheers to heavy upholstery weight. A very strong fibre which is easy to work and will take high temperatures.

Silk From the cocoon of the silk worm, silk is soft and luxurious to touch. Fades in sunlight, so protect. Available in every weight, suitable for soft furnishings, from lampshades to heavy upholstery. Good mixed with cotton or wool.

Wool A natural fibre, liable to excessive shrinkage as the 'scales' on each fibre overlap, harden and 'felt'. Is warm to touch and initially resists damp. Ideal for upholstery and curtains.

Viscose Wood pulp woven into fibres which mixes well with other fibres helping them to take dyes and fireproofing. Washable and sheds dirt easily.

FABRICS

Brocade Traditionally woven fabric using silk, cotton, wool or mixed fibres, on a jacquard loom, in a multi or self coloured floral design. Brocades drape well and can be used for curtains, traditional bed drapes, covers and upholstery. Some are washable but most will need dry cleaning.

Calico Coarse, plain weave cotton in cream or white with 'natural' flecks in it. Available in many widths and weights for inexpensive curtains, bed drapes, garden awnings. Wash before use to shrink and press while damp.

Cambric Closely woven, plain weave fabric from linen or cotton with a sheen on one side. Use, wash and press as Calico. Widely used for cushion pad covers but also for curtains, covers and cushions.

Canvas Plain weave cotton in various weights suitable for upholstered chair covers, inexpensive curtains, slip covers, awnings and outdoor use. Available as unbleached, coarse cotton or more finely woven and dyed in strong colours.

Chintz Cotton fabric with Eastern design using flowers and birds, often with a resin finish which gives a characteristic sheen or glaze and which also repels dirt. The glaze will eventually wash out, so only dry clean curtains. Avoid using steam to press and never fold or the glaze will crack.

Corduroy A strong fabric woven to form vertical ribs by floating extra yarn across which is then cut to make the pile. Use for traditional upholstery. Press on a velvet pinboard while damp.

Crewel Plain or hopsack woven, natural cotton background embroidered in chain stitch in plain cream wool or multi-coloured wools. Soft but heavy, lovely for curtains, soft blinds, cushions and light-use loose covers. May be washed, but test a small piece first.

Damask A jacquard fabric first woven in Damascus with satin floats on a warp satin background in cotton, silk, wool and mixed fibres in various weights. Use for curtains, drapes and sometimes covers and upholstery, choosing different weights for different uses. Make up reversed if a matt finish is required. Suitable for curtaining which needs to be seen from both sides.

Gingham Plain weave fabric with equal width stripes of white plus one other colour in both warp and weft threads to produce blocks of checks or stripes in 100% cotton. Use for small windows in cottagey rooms, kitchens, children's bedrooms and slip covers. Mix with floral patterns and other checks and stripes.

Holland Firm, hardwearing fabric made from cotton or linen stiffened with oil or shellac. Used for blinds lightweight covers, curtaining and pelmets.

Lace Open work fabrics in designs ranging from simple spots to elaborate panels. Usually in cotton or a cotton and polyester mixture.

Moiré A finish usually on silk or acetate described as 'watermarked'. The characteristic moiré markings are produced by pressing plain woven fabric through hot engraved cylinders which crush the threads and push them into different directions to form the pattern. This finish will disappear on contact with water, so it is not suitable for upholstery.

Muslin White or off-white, inexpensive, open-weave cloth which can be dyed in pastel colours. Used for under-curtains and sheers in hot countries to filter light and insects.

Organdie The very finest cotton fabric with an acid finish giving it a unique crispness. Use for lightweight curtains, dressing tables and lampshades. Wash and press while damp.

Organza Similar to organdie and made of silk, polyester or viscose. Very springy and used for stiffening headings of fine fabrics, blinds to filter sunlight and to protect curtains. Use layers of varying tones or pastel colours over each other.

Provençal prints Small print designs printed by hand on to fine cotton for curtains, upholstery, cushions and covers. Washable, hard wearing, soft and easy to work with.

Silk noil Light to mediumweight silk, relatively inexpensive for interlining heavy curtains, slip covers, summer curtains and cushions.

Silk shantung Light to mediumweight silk woven with irregular yarns giving a dull, rough appearance. Use for curtains, cushions, light drapes and lampshades. Available in an extensive range of colours, gathers and frills.

Taffeta Woven from silk, acetate and blends. Used for elaborate drapes because it handles well and for its light-reflecting qualities.

Tartan Authentic tartans belong to individual Scottish clans and are woven or worsted fine twill weave with an elaborate checked design. Traditional wool tartans are hardwearing for upholstering sofas and chairs, curtains and cushions.

Ticking Characteristic original herringbone weave in black and white, now woven in many colours and weights. Use for curtains and upholstery. Not usually pre-shrunk.

Toile de jouy Pastoral designs in one colour printed on to calico using copper plate printing techniques. Use for curtains, covers, upholstery, cushions and bedding.

Tweed Wool or worsted cloth in square or rectangular checked designs in few colours. Often used for shawls or more tightly woven for men's sporting clothes. However, use for upholstering stools, chairs, sofas or for curtains, pelmets and cushions.

Velvet Originally 100% silk, now made from cotton, viscose or other manmade fibres. Woven with a warp pile and additional yarn in loops which are up to 3 mm (1/8 in) depth to form a pile. Care needs to be taken when sewing or the fabrics will 'walk'. Press on a velvet pinboard. Dry clean carefully. Always buy good quality velvet with a dense pile which will not pull out easily.

Voile Fine, light plain weave cotton or polyester fabric dyed in many plain colours. Use for filmy curtains, bed drapes and under-curtains. Easily washable and little pressing necessary. Silk and wool voiles can be used for fine drapery.

FABRIC CARE

Test a piece of fabric first for shrinkage and decide whether to wash before making up or to allow the shrinkage allowance.

It is always advisable to choose washable fabrics for furnishings which will be in constant use – especially window seats and scatter cushions.

The regular removal of dust is vital to prevent particles of household dust settling into the fabric grain, as once dirt has penetrated it is very difficult to remove with any satisfaction.

Vacuum all soft furnishings regularly with a soft brush, paying special attention to the inside of the chair seats, pleats and frills. For delicate fabrics and pelmets make a muslin or fine calico 'mob cap', elasticated to fit over the end of the brush to soften the bristle/fabric abrasion.

Remove dust from cushions daily. Really bash the pad from each side between your fists or drop each cushion onto the floor one corner at a time to knock air back in, dust out, and the feathers back into the corners. Hang cushions in a cotton bag outside on a warm spring day with a light breeze to freshen fabrics and feather pads.

Small furnishings, eg silk cushions, will need to be dry cleaned at regular intervals, so use a specialist furnishings dry cleaner and clean before dirt is ingrained.

Clean interlined curtains only when disaster strikes or before alterations. Regular care and attention will prevent curtains from becoming 'dirty'. Home care kits are available for specific stains and can be used successfully on most fabrics.

INDEX